Eaton Hall · Chester
CH4 9ET

Dame Cicely Saunders founded the Hospice movement in the mid 1940's and it has been developed by volunteers giving their time, effort and money to build Hospices and then continuing to raise funds to maintain and run them.

This cookery book was initially compiled to raise funds for The Nightingale House Hospice in Wrexham and it has proved so popular that it has been re-printed for the benefit of Hospices throughout the UK from as far north as Lancashire right down to the south of England.

Each cookery book sold raises approximately £4 for the Hospice. Fund raising is an on-going struggle and by purchasing this cookery book you will be contributing towards the survival of the Hospice movement.

Natalia Westminster

THE DUCHESS OF WESTMINSTER

Introduction

Recipes and cooking have been my life-long hobby, from helping my mother cater for the holiday makers in our farmhouse in Devon, to running an outside catering business for thirty years, sixteen of which my husband, Norman, and I owned and ran Venners Restaurant in Hope.

It was during this period of time that many people asked me for recipes, or even asked me to compile a cookery book including some of my recipes. So last year when I underwent radical surgery to stop the spread of cancer, I was advised to take up a project to occupy my time. Having just retired, I thought now was the time to compile and produce my cookery book, and donate the proceeds to Nightingale House Hospice, Wrexham.

It has taken nearly a year for me to bring this book to fruition. It is divided into four sections, the first consisting of recipes from the professionals and I would particularly like to thank Dai Davies ('Dai the Chef'), former Captain of the Welsh Team for his help and assistance. The second section contains recipes from my friends to whom I owe a debt of gratitude. The recipes in the third section are from national and international celebrities whom I must also thank for taking the time and trouble to write to me with their favourite recipe. The fourth section is a collection of some of my favourite menus and recipes which I am sure you will all enjoy.

I would also like to thank my family, Norman, Ian, Amanda, Paul and Julie for their help and support, and especially my friend, Chris Tudor, for typing several of the menus. Also thanks to Alister Williams of Bridge Books for all the help and advice he gave me during the compilation of this book.

Pat Venner

Contents

Professionals

Amateurs

Celebrities

Pat Venner

Potato and Lentil Pie
(see p.15)

Professionals

Pineapple Dewi Sant

Served on a bed of cottage cheese finished with a raspberry coulis

1 pineapple	1 tbls of honey
8oz cottage cheese	4 chives
1 punnet of raspberries	

Skin the pineapple and slice into 4. Remove the centre. Thinly slice a rondel off each one. Make an incision in the rondel. Roll into a flower. Place back into the remaining four slices so that it looks like a daffodil.

For the coulis: Place the raspberries, honey and water into a pan and cook until softened, approximately 2 minutes. Drain and allow to cool

To Assemble: Using a ring cutter, place the cottage cheese into the centre of the plates. Remove top. Pour around sauce and garnish with chives.

Roast Cannon of Welsh Lamb served on a Ratatouille Gateau topped with a Ravioli of Welsh Leeks & Soft Cheese finished with a Thyme scented crust

(Serves four)

For the gateau:	1 small aubergine	2 shallots
	2 courgettes	1 clove of garlic
	3 baby peppers — yellow/red/green	Salt/peppers
	1 lb plum tomatoes (de-seeded and blanched)	Oil for cooking
For the Lamb:	2 best ends of lamb	6 ozs breadcrumbs
	1 tbls of grain mustard	1 tbls chopped fresh thyme
For the Ravioli:	9 ozs plain flour	Pinch of salt
	2 eggs	4 tsp olive oil
	2 egg yolks	

For the Leek Filling: 2 ozs Welsh goats' cheese.   Seasoning
                              6 ozs chopped leeks — blanched then dried.

For ravioli: place all the dry ingredients into a food processor and blend gradually adding the eggs and oil. Remove and wrap in cling film. Chill for 30 mins.

For the filling: finely chop the leeks and blanch in salted water for approx 2 minutes then dry on kitchen paper.

For the lamb: remove the bones, trim away all fat. Lightly season. Chill for 10 minutes. Seal in hot oil until brown then place in a medium oven for approx 8 minutes. Remove and rest on kitchen towel. Brush with mustard and top with crust.

For the ratatouille: place a little oil in pan and sweat the onions and peppers. After salting the aubergines wash and dice. Add to the onions along with the courgettes, the tomatoes and garlic. Cook until tender (approx 12 minutes). Remove & correct the seasoning.

For the pasta: roll out in the pasta machine. Place the leeks in the centre; brush the edges with water, top with the lid and cook in salted water adding a little oil.

To assemble: Place the courgettes in a gateau mould, remove sleeve, top with ravioli, fan around the lamb. Drizzle with olive oil and serve.

Blueberry & Blackcurrant Mead Pudding topped with a Quenelle of Rachel's organic Yoghurt perfumed with Vanilla

10 slices of white bread (crusts removed)
3 punnets of blueberries
2 tbls Welsh honey
4 measures of blackcurrant mead
1 tub of Rachel's Yoghurt, vanilla flavour
Few sprigs of mint

Line 4 teacups with the sliced bread that has been soaked in mead. Slightly bruise the blueberries. Add the Welsh honey and place into the pan for 2 minutes on medium heat. Allow to cool. Fill the cups with the mixture press firmly with your hand. Place into the fridge for 2 days. Remove from cups and place in the centre of a plate. Add a good tablespoon of yoghurt and garnish with a sprig of mint and serve.

Carrot Soup

Taken from a *Receipt Book 1765*, the second oldest Erddig cookery book.

2 ozs butter
2 large onions
2 large potatoes
2 lbs carrots
$^{1}/_{2}$ lb turnips
$^{1}/_{2}$ head celery
$^{1}/_{4}$ lettuce
$3^{1}/_{2}$ pts vegetable stock
Salt and pepper to taste

Peel and chop all the vegetables, melt the butter. Fry the onion add the potatoes and stir well. Add the rest of the vegetables and stock, bring to the boil and simmer. Liquidise when cooked, check for seasoning.

Welsh Lamb Casserole

2 lbs Welsh lamb	2 tbls pearl barley
2 large leeks	4 pts of lamb stock
2 large carrots	1 tbls of thyme
2 onions	

Fry off lamb, onions and leeks in a little oil. Add carrots and lamb stock. Bring to the boil and add thyme. Simmer for approximately 1 hour. Add pearl barley and simmer for a further 20–30 minutes.

Potato and Lentil Pie

2 lbs potatoes	$^{1}/_{4}$ tsp cayenne pepper
1 large onion — chopped	$^{1}/_{2}$ pt vegetable stock
2 tbls vegetable oil	4 tbls milk
8 ozs carrots — diced	1 oz butter
1 green pepper — diced	4 tbls pesto sauce
6 ozs red split lentils	4 ozs cheddar cheese — grated
1 x (400 gms) can chopped tomatoes	

Cook the potatoes, drain well. Fry the onion for about 5 minutes, add the carrots, pepper and lentils, stir for a few minutes. Add the stock, bring to the boil, reduce heat, cover and simmer until lentils are tender. Mash the potatoes with the milk and butter, season and stir in the pesto. Divide the lentil mixture between 4 individual dishes or 1 large dish. Top with the potato and sprinkle the cheese on top.

George IV Pudding

From Victoria Cust's manuscript cookery book, begun in 1839. A very rich cold pudding made with Welsh cream, fresh eggs and lemons, baked in a deep shortcrust pastry case.

1 lb shortcrust pastry	8 ozs caster sugar
$2^{1}/_{2}$ pts milk	2 lemons
$^{1}/_{4}$ pt single cream	1 pinch of nutmeg
9 eggs	

Preheat oven to 150°C. Line a 10-inch spring-form tin with the pastry. Finely grate rind of two lemons. Whisk the eggs, add the milk and cream, continue whisking whilst adding the sugar and lemon rind. Sieve the custard into the pastry case being careful not to spill over the sides of the pastry. Sprinkle over a pinch of nutmeg. Place on a baking sheet and bake towards the bottom of the oven for about 1–1$^{1}/_{2}$hrs until just set. Leave to cool and refrigerate.

French Onion Tarts

Serves 8. A wonderful thin herb cheese pastry filled with a classic onion and olive mixture. Make these in two Yorkshire pudding tins, each will make four individual tarts.

Herb and Cheese Pastry:

6 ozs (150 gms) plain flour

$^1/_4$ tsp salt

1 tsp mustard powder

3 ozs (75 gms) butter (cut into small pieces 2 ozs/50 gms)

2 ozs Parmesan — grated

1 tbls fresh thyme leaves

1 large egg, beaten

Filling:

1 large Spanish onion — thinly sliced

1 tablespoon olive oil

1 clove garlic — crushed

4 ozs (100 gms) gruyere cheese — grated

1 large handful parsley — coarsely chopped

2 large eggs

$^1/_2$ pt (300 mls) double cream

salt and black pepper

12 black stoned olives — halved

Pre-heat oven to gas mark 7 (220°C/425°F) and put in a heavy baking sheet to get hot. First make the pastry. Measure the flour, salt, mustard, thyme and butter into the processor or a bowl, rub in process until the mixture resembles fine breadcrumbs. Add the parmesan and the beaten egg and mix again just as long as it takes for the ingredients to come together. Chill for 30 minutes wrapped in cling film. Heat the oil in a pan and cook the onion on high heat for a few minutes. Lower the temperature and cover, allow to cook until soft. Return to high heat and add the garlic. Roll the pastry thinly on a lightly floured work surface and using a $4^3/_4$-inch (11.5 cms) cutter, cut out 8 discs. Use these to line two Yorkshire pudding trays. Chill if time allows. Divide the cold onion between the tartlet cases, top with the grated cheese and roughly chopped parsley. Beat the eggs and add the double cream and seasoning. Carefully pour the egg and cream mixture into the tartlets, top each with a few halved olives. Bake in the pre-heated oven on the hot baking sheet for 15–20 minutes, turning around half way through the cooking time, until set and pale golden. Serve warm as a first course or a light lunch with salad.

Chicken Breasts with Sage and Orange Marinade

Serves 6. A quick recipe — good enough for dinner party or for family supper, no extra sauce needs to be made as the marinade is the sauce.

6 chicken breasts — skin on

Few sprigs of fresh sage

Marinade:

2 cloves garlic — crushed

1 dessertspoon coarsely grated fresh ginger

$^1/_2$ pt (300 mls) orange juice from a packet

1 tbls olive oil

3 tbls soy sauce

1 tbls dried sage

Coffee and Brandy Gateaux
(see p.63)

Pre-heat oven to gas mark 7 (425°F/220°C). Combine the marinade ingredients and put with the chicken breasts into two plastic bags or large freezer bags, one inside the other, to marinade. Marinate for about 24 hours in the fridge. Remove the chicken from the marinade, arrange the breasts, skin side up in a large roasting tin and roast for about 20 minutes. Pour the marinade over the chicken and return to the oven for 5-10 minutes or until the juices run clear. Remove from the oven and arrange the chicken in a serving dish. Strain the juices and serve separately. Decorate with fresh sage and serve.

Iced Lemon Flummery

Serves about 12. A wonderfully refreshing dessert and light too — perfect for after Christmas.

$^1/_2$ pt (300 mls) double cream	12 ozs (350 gms) caster sugar
Finely grated rind and juice of 2 lemons	1 pt (600 mls) milk

To serve: Pour cream into a bowl and whisk until it forms soft peaks. Stir in the lemon rind, juice, sugar and milk and mix well until thoroughly blended. Pour into a $2^1/_2$ pint (1.5 litre) shallow plastic container, cover with lid and freeze for at least 8 hours — or preferably overnight — until firm. Remove from freezer and cut into chunks and mix in a processor until smooth and creamy. Pour into 12 small ramekin dishes, cover with cling film and return to the freezer until required. Remove from the freezer about 15 minutes ahead and spoon or pipe a blob of the whipped cream on top of each ramekin, decorate with a sprig of mint or slices of strawberry.

To prepare ahead and freeze: Freeze in ramekins — remove from freezer about 15 mins before serving so they begin to soften.

Roasted Red Pepper, Aubergine and Ricotta Terrine

Serves 8.

8 large red peppers	750 mls white wine vinegar
1 block fetta — crumbled	4 tsp sugar
250g ricotta	4 cloves garlic
2 tsp toasted pinenuts	1 tsp salt
1 tsp finely shredded basil	1 tsp whole black peppercorns
$^3/_4$ cup breadcrumbs	3 blades mace — optional
4 medium aubergines — sliced lengthways and salted	Olive oil

Top and seed the peppers and place on an oven tray under a hot grill until they start to blacken. Remove to a bowl and cover. tightly with cling film until cold. In a pan, boil the vinegar, peppercorns, mace, sugar, garlic and salt for five minutes and cool. Strain and reserve the liquid. In another bowl ,combine the ricotta, fetta, pinenuts, breadcrumbs and season well. Peel the peppers and reserve. Rinse the aubergine slices and pat dry.

Fry the slices in batches in a little olive oil and drain. When all fried, marinate them in the vinegar mixture for 30 minutes.

To assemble, take a loaf tin or similar and line with cling film. Carefully line with red peppers, then aubergine slices and pack with half the ricotta mixture. Add a layer of peppers, use up all the ricotta and finish with aubergine and peppers. Weight it down overnight. Serve with a few leaves and balsamic vinagrette.

Whole Boned Chicken with Parsley Pesto and Apricot Stuffing

1.35 kg free range chicken, boned (get your butcher to do this)
2 large chicken breasts
4 thin slices of Parma ham
1 large glass of dry white wine
1 tbls olive oil

150 mls home-made pesto
150 gms pecans
150 gms ready to use dried apricots
Salt and pepper

Pre-heat the oven to gas mark 6 (200°C/400°F). Spread half the pesto on the inside of the flattened carcass of the boned bird. Wrap the chicken breasts in 2 of the slices of Parma trim and place these centrally on the pesto. Now spread the remaining pesto on top of them. Arrange the pecans and apricots over the bird and push firmly into the bird, working into the legs and between the breasts. Wrap the boned bird around these to make a neat joint. Put the joint in a terrine or 900 gms/2 lbs loaf tin. Pour around the wine, brush the breasts of the bird with the olive oil and season with salt and pepper. Then cover loosely with foil. Roast for 1$\frac{1}{2}$ hours, removing the foil and basting after 1 hour. Baste again 20 minutes later. Remove from the oven and leave to cool in the tin or dish, then refrigerate overnight. Remove from the tin, place on a board and cut across into slices about 2.5cm/1-inch thick. Drizzle with a little extra-virgin olive oil and serve with a wedge of lemon and mayonnaise thinned with the skimmed cooking juices.

Apricot and Frangipane Tart

Serves 8, with ice cream or crème fraiche.

Pastry;
250 gms plain flour
125 gms butter
1 egg

10 gms caster sugar
5 gms salt
40 mls (approximately) water

Filling:
12 ripe apricots

Frangipane cream: 3 eggs
250 gms unsalted butter
250 gms icing sugar

250 gms ground almonds
50 gms flour
2 tbls maraschino

Blend the pastry ingredients in a food processor until they form a ball, roll thinly and line a deep 8-inch/21 cms tin. Rest pastry case in the fridge for 2 hours; then bake blind in a preheated oven 180°C. Meanwhile, halve and stone the apricots. To make the almond cream, beat the butter until fluffy and mix the sugar and almonds together. Mix into the butter and then add the flour. Add the eggs, one at a time, and then add the Maraschino. Spread the almond cream into the pastry case and arrange the apricot halves over the cream. Bake for about 45 minutes, until the cream has set. Cool and dust with icing sugar.

Jubby Pie

2 tbls vegetable oil
1 medium onion — finely chopped
1 medium leek — pale or green part only — sliced
200 gms/7 ozs turkey or chicken mince —
    no skin or fat
50 gms/ 2 ozs frozen peas
1 small carrot — finely chopped
1 stick celery — finely chopped

6 tbls tomato ketchup
150 mls/5 fl ozs chicken stock — boiling
Salt and freshly ground black pepper
750 gms/1$\frac{1}{2}$ lbs warm mashed potatoes —with
    butter and milk added but not too loose
2 tbls flour
Unsalted butter
Melted grated cheese — optional

Heat the vegetable oil in a pan until sizzling. Add the onion and leek and cook for 5 minutes to soften. Add the turkey, peas, carrot and celery and cook for a futher 10 minutes. Next add the flour and ketchup, and mix well, then add the boiling stock and bring to the boil, stirring all the time. Cook for 10 minutes, or until the vegetables are cooked. Place the whole lot into a food processor and blitz until smooth. Spoon into a bowl. Place a layer of mashed potato in the bottom of an ovenproof dish — make sure you use plenty of potato. Top with pureed mixture — finely puréed, in thin layers. Repeat until the dish is full, finishing with a topping of potato. Cover the top of the potato well with the melted butter and cook in a preheated oven at gas mark 7 (220°C/435°F) for 25 minutes until the top is nicely browned and crunchy. If the kids like cheese, then top with the cheese before glazing. Serve hot with green peas or sweetcorn. This dish can also be made in batches and freezes perfectly — just defrost and reheat in a moderate oven.

Chocolate and Banana Strudel with Ice Cream

Serves 4-6. Simple, tasty pudding. Preparation time: 15 minutes. Cooking time: 30 minutes.

90 g /3$\frac{1}{4}$ ozs pecan nuts — roughly chopped
3 ripe large bananas — cubed roughly
6 large sheets of filo pastry
75 gms/2$\frac{3}{4}$ ozs unsalted butter
Melted chocolate ice cream — to serve

25 gms/1 ozs white chocolate —
    roughly chopped
Finely grated zest of 1 large lime
75 gms/2$\frac{3}{4}$ ozs bitter chocolate —
    roughly chopped

Preheat the oven to gas mark 7 (220°C). Place the nuts, bananas, lime zest and chocolates into a bowl and stir well. Lay a tea towel on the worktop and lay one sheet of filo on top. Brush some of the melted butter over the filo, then add another layer of pastry and repeat until all six have been buttered. Leaving a 5 cm border of pastry, spoon the filling onto one end of the pastry then fold over the top end of the filo to enclose. Using the tea towel, roll up the strudel. Tuck each end under and place on a nonstick baking tray. Butter well and bake in the oven for about 30 minutes, or until golden and crisp. Remove from the oven and leave to cool for 10 minutes, then cut with a serrated knife on a slight angle. Top with good quality chocolate ice cream.

Asparagus Bread and Butter Pudding

12 rounds bread and butter	300 mls cream
300 gms asparagus spears	2 large eggs
150 gms parmesan cheese	Salt and pepper
6 Spring onions	Grated nutmeg
1 or 2 cloves garlic	A handful of walnuts pieces — optional

Cook the asparagus for just 3 minutes in boiling, salted water. Chop and sauté the onions and the garlic in a little oil until just softened. Line a buttered ovenproof dish with the bread and butter. Add a layer of asparagus and the onion mix. Cover with shavings of parmesan — shavings can be done with the potato peeler. Season and put another layer of bread and butter and the remaining vegetables on top. Finish off with more parmesan and the walnuts if you want to include them. Whisk together the cream and the eggs and pour over the other ingredients in the dish. Allow to stand for at least $1/2$ an hour. Grate over a little nutmeg and cook until lightly golden brown with crispy edges and a slightly soft centre. Serve with a good crisp well-dressed salad.

Aga cook on the grid shelf on the floor of the roasting oven for 20 minutes. Electric cook in the fan oven at gas mark 6 (170°C) for 20–30 minutes. Combination oven cook at 200°C with 360 watt microwave for 10–15 minutes.

Stilton Stuffed Chicken Breast

4 boneless chicken breasts

Stuffing: 80-100 gms stilton cheese	1 tsp chopped thyme
2 slices of bread — made into breadcrumbs	40 gms walnut pieces — chopped — optional
40 gms cottage cheese	Salt and black pepper
2 spring onions — chopped	Butter or oil
1 tbs chopped parsley	Wine or water

Wipe and trim the chicken breasts, (you can make this dish with the skin either on or off the joints). Place the breast between two layers of cling film and beat out to make a larger flat piece of chicken. Mash together all the stuffing ingredients, the walnuts are optional as not everyone can eat nuts. Spread a thin layer of the filling over each flattened chicken breast and roll it up and roll it up in cling film to hold its shape and

Aunty Emma Cake
(see p.64)

refrigerate for several hours or freeze, this allows you to just remove as many as required when necessary. Oil or butter an ovenproof dish or roasting tin and place the chicken in this, (if the skin has been removed put a little oil or butter on each piece of chicken). Pour about 50 mls of wine or water into the base of the dish and bake.

Aga on the bottom set of runners in the roasting oven for 20–30 mins and until the juices run clear. Electric fan oven, gas mark 6 (170°C) for 20-30 mins depending on the size of the joints and until the juices run clear. Combination oven, 180°C with 360 watt for 15-20 mins.

Remove the chicken from the dish. Add a little more wine or water to the dish and loosen the sediment, then pour into a saucepan. Reheat and reduce if necessary, or thicken with 1 tsp cornflour mixed with a drop of water and added to the boiling liquid, stirring as it thickens. Pour over the chicken. Serve on mashed potato with wholegrain mustard added and sugar snap peas.

Blackcurrant Syllabub

400 gms blackcurrants
100 gms sugar
100 mls rosé wine
70 gms caster sugar

Juice of a small lemon
250 mls double cream
A few toasted flaked almonds

Prepare the blackcurrants and rinse in a colander. Put in a saucepan and add the sugar. Heat gently and simmer very gently for 20 minutes and then allow to cool. Put the wine, caster sugar and lemon juice in a bowl and chill overnight. Stir well and then add the cream and whip until light and fluffy. Put 2 tbs of the blackcurrants in a wine glass and top with syllabub. Finish with a sprinkling of flaked almonds. Serve with biscotti!

Biscotti

250 gms plain flour
$^{1}/_{2}$ tsp baking powder
150 gms caster sugar
65 gms butter
$^{1}/_{2}$ tsp almond essence

2 eggs
50 gms pistachio nuts
100 gms whole hazelnuts — toasted
A little extra caster sugar

Put the flour, caster sugar, baking powder and the butter (cut up) in the food processor and mix to the breadcrumb stage. Add the almond essence and the eggs and process until it binds together. Turn out onto a floured board and knead in the whole nuts. Line a baking tray with bake-o-glide. Shape the dough into a sausage about 30-35 cm long, put on the baking tray and flatten slightly and bake.

Aga cook in the baking oven for 30 minutes on the third set of runners. Alternatively, cook in the roasting oven on the bottom set of runners. Put the cold shelf above after 10 minutes and cook 10 more minutes.

Electric fan oven: cook at gas mark 5 (160°C) for 30 minutes until golden. Remove from the oven and leave to cool for 20 minutes. Cut up into 1-2 cm thick slices, replace on the baking tray and return to the oven. Bake Aga: cook in the simmering oven for 30 minutes. Electric fan oven: cook at gas mark 3 (150°C) for 30 minutes until it is dried out.

The biscotti are a good contrast to syllabub, but are also excellent for coffee dunking!

Thai Style Crab Cakes (Starter)

^{1}/2 kilo of white fish trimmings
2 medium eggs
130 mls of double cream
1 tsp of grated ginger
1^1/2 red chillies — sliced thinly
1^1/2 tbls of Thai fish sauce

2 tbls of chopped coriander
1^1/2 tbls of cornflour
1 tsp of salt
1 bunch of spring onions (chopped finely)
75 gms of white crab meat

Purée fish trimmings in food blender, add the eggs one at a time, then slowly add the cream. Add the rest of the ingredients. Roll into 20 mm pieces, then deep fry until cooked.

Braised Lamb Shank on Hot Pot Vegetables and Creamed Parsnips

Serves 6. Main Course

6 lamb shanks
4 carrots
2 onions
3 leeks
^{1}/2 a swede diced
1 head of garlic
Rosemary and thyme
Half a bottle of red wine

2 bay leaves
12 black pepper corns
1 kilo of parsnips
2 potatoes
100 mls of double cream
50 gms of butter
2 litres of either demi glaze or gravy

Season the lamb shanks, then seal them off in a hot deep roasting tray until you have browned them on all sides. Add the chopped vegetables, herbs, garlic, bay leaves and pepper corns. Make sure the vegetables have browned. Add the red wine, then the gravy until the lamb shanks are covered. Cover with tin foil then braise them in a moderate oven for 1^1/2-2 hours (or until the meat is nearly falling off the bone). Meanwhile dice the parsnips and the potatoes and cook all the way through. Drain off the mash, add the cream and butter, and season. Then on the plate place the shank on top of the mash. Place the diced vegetables around the plate. Strain off the cooking liquor and pour over the lamb shank. Pickled red cabbage is also a good accompaniment.

Raspberry Ripple Cheesecake

5 portions. Dessert

225 gms cream cheese
112 gms caster sugar
300 mls whipped cream
65 gms unsalted butter

150 gms digested biscuits
80 mls raspberry purée
10 raspberries

Melt butter, crush biscuits and mix together. Whip the cream and mix the cream cheese and sugar together. Fold in the whipped cream into the cream cheese mix. Layer up in a individual small cutter or ring mould in following order: Biscuit base; cheese mixture: raspberry purée. Repeat 3 times until you have reached the top of the mould. Smooth over with a palate knife. Leave to set for 1–1¹/₂ hours. Push the bottom of the biscuit base up carefully until the cheesecake comes out of the mould. Place on a plate and garnish with raspberries and mint.

Baked Aubergine Parmigana Served with Ciabatta

Serves 6.

2 large aubergines
500 mls tomato passata
2 buffalo mozzarella balls
Fresh parmesan — grated finely

Fresh basil
Olive oil
Flat leaf parsley
1 ciabatta loaf

This is a very simple yet tasty starter with a good quality tomato passata — the most important ingredient. Trim your aubergines and slice lengthways approximately 1 cm thick and griddle with olive oil on a high heat until tender. In a fairly large baking dish simply layer the tomato, basil and aubergines and break the buffalo mozzarella into pieces and spread evenly over the top. Add your parmesan, parsley and bake until golden brown and bubbly. Serve with crusty ciabatta.

Steak Diane My Way

Serves 4.

4 x 10 ozs best sirloin steaks
Garlic clove — sliced
Butter
Paprika
French mustard

Salt and black pepper
500 mls good red wine
350 mls whipping cream
1 large onion — sliced
4 large field mushrooms — sliced

First dress the steaks — each with 1 tbls mustard, good pinch of parika, salt and pepper. In a large frying pan on high heat add a large knob of butter, onions and garlic. When caramelised add the mushrooms and push to

Salmon en Croûte
(see p. 82)

the side of the pan. Add a little more butter and the steaks seasoned side down. Seal and turn, now add the wine and simmer for 5 minutes before adding the cream. Simmer for a further 5 minutes until the sauce has thickened. Serve with your preferred choice of potatoes and vegetables. I like to serve a delicious creamy mash with fresh spinach.

Ricotta Cheesecake with Fresh Cream

500 gms digestives
100 gms melted butter
Fresh ricotta
350 mls double cream

Fresh fruit of your choice (I prefer
  strawberries or raspberries)
Sugar

Simply place the biscuits in a blender and add the melted butter. Remove and line a cake tin and place in freezer to set. Remove from freezer after 30 minutes. Mix ricotta with a little sugar and place in base. Top with fruits and double whipped cream and enjoy. It is also fantastic with a shot of amaretto over!

Open Apple Tart

For 2 lbs of hard sweet apples (not cooking apples), peeled and cored, evenly and thinly sliced, melt 2 ozs of butter in a large frying pan. Put in the apples. Add 3 or 4 tbls of white sugar and 1 or 2 tbls of water. Cook gently until the apples are pale golden and transparent. Turn the slices over very gently so as not to break them, and if they are closely packed, shake the pan rather than stir the apples. Remove from the heat. (You can cook the apples in water instead of butter, but the scent of apples cooking in butter is worth the extra calories!

While the apples are cooking, make a pâté sablée — or crumbly pastry, by rubbing 3 ozs of butter into 6 ozs of plain flour, a $1/4$ tsp of salt and 3 tsps of white sugar. Moisten with 2–4 tbls of chilled water, but the less water you use the more crumbly and light your pastry will be.

Now comes the easy bit: simply shape the pastry into a ball and immediately, without leaving it to rest or even rolling it out, spread it with your hands into a lightly buttered 8-inch flan tin. Brush the edges with cream or milk; arrange the apples, without the juice, in overlapping circles, keeping a nicely-shaped piece for the centre. Bake, with the tin on a baking sheet, in a preheated hot oven at gas mark 6, (400°F) for 30–35 minutes, turning the tin round once during the cooking. Take it from the oven, pour over the juices, which have been reheated, give another sprinkling of sugar and return to the oven for barely a minute.

Pork and Chive Sausage and Kidney in Red Wine and Mushroom Sauce

Serves 4. Preparation time: 20 minutes; cooking time 40-50 minutes.

450g (1 lb) pork and chive sausage	150 mls (1/4 pt) beef stock
8 lambs kidneys	150 mls (1/4 pt) red wine
25 gms (1 oz) seasoned flour	2 tablespoons tomato purée
2 tablespoons vegetable oil	2 bay leaves
8 button mushrooms	Salt and ground black pepper
Large onion — peeled	

Skin the kidneys and cut them in half. Snip out the central white core with scissors and then toss them in the seasoned flour. Heat the oil in a frying pan and gently fry the onions and mushrooms until pale golden. Add the kidneys and sausages and fry until browned all over. Stir in the stock, red wine, tomato purée and bay leaves. Bring to the boil and then reduce to a simmer. Cover and cook over a gentle heat for 40–50mins or until the sausages and kidneys are cooked. Check the seasoning and serve immediately. Serve with creamy mashed potatoes and seasonal veg.

Pan Fried Sirloin Buffalo Steak with Buffalo Soft Cheese and Pumpkin Vegetable Cake

Serves 4.

4 buffalo sirloin steaks	100 gms grated carrots
200 gms buffalo	500 mls beer
Soft fresh cheese	250 mls strong beef stock
250 gms potatoes	1 wine glass red wine
300 gms pumpkin	(Other vegetables can be used if desired e.g.
200 gms cabbage	turnip, onion, leek)

Trim and pan fry the steak to seal then place the sliced buffalo cheese on the top and glaze under the grill. Peel and dice the potato and boil until soft. Shred and blanch the cabbage. Strain and mash the potatoes and pumpkin and add the blanched cabbage and grated carrot. Mould the vegetables into four cakes and fry until golden brown. Reduce the red wine, add the beef stock and the beer and reduce to a sauce. Place the vegetable cake on the plate and place the steak on top and pour the sauce around.

Amateurs

Chicken Liver Paté

1 lb chicken livers	1 tbls brandy
$^1/_2$ lb unsmoked streaky bacon	2 cloves garlic
1 medium size onion	Ground pepper
1 hard boiled egg	Pinch of ground cloves, ginger and cinnamon
$^1/_2$ lb butter	

Sauté the finely chopped onion in $2^1/_2$ ozs of the butter until transparent and soft, add the chopped up bacon. When cooked remove the bacon and onion and put aside. Add $2^1/_2$ ozs more butter and the chicken livers and fry them for 7 minutes until they are pink but not bloody. Chop up the hard boiled egg and put all the ingredients in a liquidiser until thoroughly blended. Put into a dish or ramekin and when partially set melt the last 3 ozs butter and pour over the top to seal. Chill in the fridge or freeze.

Butternut Squash Soup

1 butternut squash	2 tbls honey
2 tablespoon olive oil	100 gms ground almonds
1 medium white onion — chopped roughly	$^1/_4$ tin coconut milk
1-2 cloves garlic — crushed	1 pt vegetable stock
Zest and juice of 2-3 limes	Salt and pepper to taste

Halve the squash, scoop out and discard the pulp and seeds at the centre. Peel the squash and cut into chunks. Heat the oil, then add the onion and a little salt. Fry gently for 3 minutes or so, then add the garlic and fry for a minute more before adding the squash. Fry the vegetables for a couple more minutes, stirring. Pour on the vegetable stock, bring to the boil, then turn down to a simmer and cover the pan. Cook for 20 minutes or until the squash is tender — test with a fork. Add the lime zest and juice, the honey and the ground almonds and then liquidise until the soup is smooth. Finally, stir in the coconut milk and season the soup to taste. Reheat gently if necessary.

Family Cheese and Onion Pie

Prepare about 6 to 8 fairly large potatoes and add salt to them. Boil them in a large pan. Separately cook an onion (sliced fairly finely) in a small amount of water to soften it. I do this in the microwave for about 4-5 minutes. Dry the potatoes. Add the pepper, the cooked onions, a teaspoon of nutmeg and three tablespoons of chopped parsley. Mash the potatoes with milk and butter. Add two cupfuls of grated cheddar cheese —

strong or mature cheese gives the best flavour. Keep another cup of grated cheese nearby. Place the mixture in a buttered ovenproof dish. Top this with the remaining cup of grated cheese. Cook in the oven (about 180°C) for 20 minutes or until the cheese on the top is a good golden brown colour. Serve with crispy bacon or sausages and heated plum tomatoes.

Carrot and Cheese Flan

8-inch short crust pastry flan case.

Filling:

2 ozs margarine or butter	1 tsp chopped chives
4 ozs carrot grated	Salt
2 eggs	Freshly ground pepper
1/4 pt single cream	3 ozs mature Cheddar, grated
3 tbls milk	Parsley sprigs to garnish

Melt the margarine/butter in a saucepan. Add the carrot and cook gently for about 5 minutes. Remove from the heat and cool. Beat together the eggs, cream, milk, and chives. Add salt and pepper to taste. Stir in the carrot and pour into the prepared flan case. Sprinkle with cheese. Bake at 190°C (375°F, gas mark 5) for 30 minutes or until the filling is set and golden. Serve hot or cold and garnish with parsley.

Onion and Cheese Pie

3 medium-sized onions, finely chopped	1/2 tsp white pepper
1/2 lb of strong Cheddar cheese, grated	Pinch of nutmeg
1 egg, lightly beaten	Shortcrust pastry
2 tbls butter	10-inch/26 cm pie dish
1 tsp dry English mustard powder	

Melt the butter over a medium heat, add the chopped onion and pinch of nutmeg. Reduce heat to low and cook gently for 10° minutes — do not let onions brown. Mix the cooked onions with the grated cheese and add most of the beaten egg, keeping a little to glaze the pastry. Add the salt, pepper and dry mustard and beat well. Spread evenly over pastry base, cover with remaining pastry and brush over remaining egg. Bake at 200°C for 35 minutes. Serve hot or cold.

Watercress Roulade

200 gms watercress	2 tbls crème fraiche
4 large eggs, separated	150 gms smoked salmon (optional)
Salt and freshly ground black pepper	Squeeze lemon juice (optional)
250 gms full fat soft cheese	

Christmas Eve Cake and
Elderflower Champagne
(see p.64)

Preheat the oven to 190°C(170°C fan oven), 375°F, gas 5. Grease and line a swiss roll tin (32cm x 25cm approx) with baking parchment. Put the watercress in a food processor with the egg yolks, and season with salt and pepper. Whizz until the watercress is finely chopped. Turn into a large bowl, taking care to scrape the sides of the processor bowl with a spatula to get all the mixture out. Whisk the egg whites until stiff and then fold into the watercress mixture. Turn into the tin and level the top, making sure the mixture goes right into the corners. Bake for 15-20 minutes or until the centre springs back when lightly pressed. As soon as it comes out of the oven, cover with a clean tea towel and leave to cool. Turn out onto a clean sheet of paper and then carefully remove the lining paper in strips this helps to prevent the roulade breaking. Mix the soft cheese and crème fraiche together and spread on the roulade. Cover with smoked salmon if using and sprinkle with lemon juice. Carefully roll up as tightly as possible like a swiss roll. Wrap in cling film and refrigerate for at least 30mins. Cut into slices and serve.

Salmon en Croûte

2 x 1 lb pieces of salmon fillet
4 ozs butter — softened
4 pieces of stem ginger — chopped
1 oz currants

$1/2$ teaspoon ground mace
$1^1/2$ lb puff pastry (pre-rolled is suitable)
1 egg beaten seasoning $1/2$ tablespoon chopped dill

Season fish, mix butter, ginger, currants and dill together. Lay a piece of pastry 7 x 13 inch on to floured baking tray, put one of the fish fillets on the pastry, brush edge of pastry with beaten egg. Cover the fish with the butter mixture, and then put remaining fillet on top. Cover this with a piece of pastry just a little larger than the bottom pastry, press the pastry together well to seal it. Trim the edge neatly, brush with beaten egg, and chill for 1 hour. Preheat oven to gas mark 6 (400°F, 200°C). Brush the Salmon en Croute with egg again. Cook for 35–40 minutes.

Grilled Hake Fillets with Crispy Cheese Topping

These crisp moist fillets with a hint of garlic are lovely served with puréed spinach and new potatoes. You could use fillets of cod or haddock if hake is unavailable.

2 large or 4 small hake fillets
1 tbls sunflower oil
1 tsp garlic pureeq
4 tbls dry white wine

4 ozs (125 gms) brown bread crumbs
4 ozs(125 gms) cheddar or gruyere cheese grated
Freshly ground black pepper

Wash the fish and pat dry with kitchen paper. Leave the skin on, as this helps to keep the shape of the fillets. If you are using large fillets, cut each into two pieces. Cream the sunflower oil and garlic puree together to make a paste. Spread over the top of each fillet and sprinkle with a little freshly ground pepper. Heat the grill, remove the rack and pour in the wine — just enough to cover the base of the pan. Put the fillets skin side down in the bottom of the pan. Top each fillet with the combined breadcrumbs and grated cheese and grill for about 4–6 minutes. When crisp and golden serve on warmed plates with the cooking juices and wine poured over.

Baked Monk Fish with Crème Fraiche in Foil

(Serves 6)

6 x 200 gms pieces of monk fish fillet
2 tsp of fresh rosemary
3 garlic cloves — peeled and cut into slivers
100 gms butter — melted

Sea salt and freshly ground black pepper
6 dsp crème fraiche
6 dsp of extra dry white vermouth

Preheat oven to 200°C (400°F, gas mark 6). With a sharp knife, make tiny slits evenly all over the monkfish, and insert 2–3 rosemary leaves, a sliver of garlic and some salt and pepper halfway into each. Make six rectangles of double foil, dull side out. Brush with butter and place a piece of monkfish in the centre of one half of the foil. Put a dessertspoon of crème fraiche on top. Fold the other half of the foil over the monkfish, and then fold the sides in tightly, but leave the top open. Pour a dessert spoonful of vermouth into each 'parcel' and seal well. It is essential for the package to be airtight to stop the steam escaping. Place the foil packages on a baking tray and bake at the top of the pre-heated oven for 20 minutes. Serve immediately with the juices.

Spiced Chicken Mayonnaise

1 medium chicken or chicken pieces
4 tbls clear honey
4 tbls sweet fruit chutney
4 tsps curry powder
4 tbls white wine (or cider)

4 tbls mayonnaise
4 tbls thick whipped cream
2 ozs toasted flaked almonds
8 ozs rice (weight before boiling)

Melt the honey in a heavy pan. Stir in the curry powder and chutney and cook for ten minutes, stirring occasionally. Remove from the heat, blend in the wine and sieve to remove large pieces of chutney then leave to cool. Stir the mayonnaise and cream together then add the cool curry mixture a little at a time. Strip the meat from the chicken, cut into pieces and toss in the mayonnaise. Boil the rice as directed and when cool pile round the border of the dish with chicken mixture in centre. Garnish with green and black grapes.

Chicken and Tomato Casserole à la Joan

3-4 chicken breasts, cut into bite-size pieces
1 large onion (chopped)
1 clove garlic (crushed)
3-4 rashers of streaky bacon (rind removed and chopped)

$^1/_2$ pt white wine
$^1/_2$ pt chicken stock
2 tbls tomato purée
1 tsp sugar

2 carrots (chopped)
12 celery sticks (chopped)
1 heaped tbls of plain floor
1 tsp dried mixed herbs
Dumplings (makes about 8)
    3 ozs self-raising flour
    $1^1/2$ ozs suet
    Salt and pepper

14 ozs canned chopped tomatoes
1 bouquet garni
Salt and pepper

A little sage
Water

Fry chicken pieces in oil and place in a large casserole dish. Fry onion and bacon then add garlic, carrots, and celery, and fry. Add flour and cook for 1 minute. Pour in white wine, chicken stock and cook until thickened. Add tomatoes, tomato purée, sugar, mixed herbs, salt and pepper. Pour over chicken. Add bouquet garni. Cover and cook for 1 to $1^1/4$ hours at 375°F (190°C gas mark 5) in the centre of the oven.

Dumplings — Place all the dry ingredients in a bowl and mix. Add enough water to bind the dumplings together. Shape into walnut sized pieces. Add to the casserole 20 minutes before end of cooking time.

Spicy Tangerine Chicken Stir Fry

(Very generous helpings for 4. I usually halve the recipe)

4 chicken breasts, skinned and cut into strips
2 red peppers, de-seeded and cut into strips
1 courgette, sliced

1 onion, sliced
4 garlic cloves
3 tablespoons oil

Marinade: 1 tbls rich or dark soy sauce
    1 tbls oyster sauce

1 tbls rice wine or sherry
2 tsp or zest from a tangerine
    or orange

Wok sauce: $^1/3$ cup of tangerine or orange juice
    1 tbls oyster sauce
    2 tsp Asian chilli sauce — only use 1 if
        you do not want it too hot

$^1/4$ cup of rice wine or sherry
1 tbls cornflour (rounded)

Mix marinade ingredients together in a bowl. Place chicken pieces together into marinade and refrigerate for at least 1 hour, but not more than 8 hours. Remove the seeds from the red peppers and cut them into strips. Place the pepper strips, sliced onion & courgettes in a bowl and refrigerate for an hour or so, longer if you like.

Mix together all ingredients for the wok sauce and set aside.

Heat the wok and add 2 tablespoons of oil. When the oil gives of a wisp of smoke add the chicken. Stir and toss until it loses its raw colour. Slide onto a plate and keep in a warm oven. Add 1 more tablespoon of oil to the wok. 4 finely minced cloves of garlic and after about 5–8 seconds add all the vegetables. Cook until they

Hobnob Lemon Slice
(see p.38)

brighten in colour, about 2 minutes, possibly slightly longer. Stir the wok sauce and add it to the vegetables in the wok. Return the chicken to the wok and stir-fry until the sauce thickens enough to glaze the chicken and vegetables. Taste and adjust the seasoning. Transfer to a heated bowl or plates.

Venison Steaks with Cranberry Cumberland Sauce

Steaks:
  2 Venison steaks each about 7–8 ozs (200–225 gms) 2 medium shallots, finely chopped
  1 tbls of groundnut oil Salt
  1 dsp of crushed peppercorns

Sauce:
  2 rounded tablespoons of cranberry jelly 1 slightly rounded teaspoon of
  Zest and juice of ¹/2 large orange   mustard powder
  Zest and juice of ¹/2 small lemon 3 tbls of port
  1 tsp of freshly grated root ginger

Make the sauce way ahead of time- — preferably a couple of hours or even several days ahead — so there is time for flavours to develop. Take off the outer zest of the half orange and the lemon using a potato peeler. Then with a sharp knife shred these into really fine hairlike pieces, about 4 inch (1cm) long.

   Place the cranberry jelly, ginger and mustard in a saucepan, and add the zest and the squeezed orange and lemon juice, and place it over a medium heat. Now bring it up to simmering point, whisking well to combine everything together, then as soon as it begins to simmer turn the heat off. Stir in the port and pour it into a jug to keep till needed. When you are ready to cook the steaks, heat the oil in a medium sized, thick-based frying pan. Dry the venison thoroughly with kitchen paper, then sprinkle and press the crushed peppercorns firmly over both sides of each steak. When the oil is smoking hot, drop the steaks into the pan and let them cook for 5 minutes on each side for medium (4 mins for rare and 6 for well done). Halfway through add the shallots and move them around the pan to cook and brown at the edges. Then 30 seconds before the end of the cooking time pour in the sauce —not over but around the steaks. Let it bubble for a minute or two, season with salt, and then serve the steaks with the sauce poured over. A garnish of watercress would be nice, and a good accompaniment would be mini jacket potatoes and a mixed-leaf salad.

Cowboy Pie

  1¹/2 ozs butter 8 ozs leeks — trimmed and sliced 14 fl ozs milk
  Salt and freshly ground black pepper 12 ozs potatoes — peeled and boiled
  1 large tin baked beans in tomato sauce 8 ozs swede — peeled and boiled
  ¹/2 of a 330 gms can of corned beef— chilled and cubed 1 oz cheddar cheese — grated
  1 oz flour ¹/2 oz fresh breadcrumbs

Melt ¹/2 oz of the butter in a saucepan. Add the leeks, season, cover and cook for 5 minutes until tender. Place in an ovenproof dish with the beans and the corned beef. Place ¹/2 oz the butter, the flour and ¹/2 pint of the milk in a saucepan. Heat, whisking continuously until the sauce boils. Simmer for 3 minutes, stirring occasionally. Pour over the corned beef mix. Mash the potatoes and swede with the remaining butter and milk. Spoon carefully over the sauce. Sprinkle with the cheese and breadcrumbs and bake for 30 minutes until golden at gas mark 6 (400°F, 200°C).

David's Steak Sauce

1 oz butter
1 onion — peeled and sliced
4 ozs mushrooms — peeled and sliced.
1 red pepper — de-seeded and sliced
1 tsp mixed dried herbs or 1 tbls
    chopped fresh herbs

1 oz sultanas.
4 tbls brandy.
$^1/_4$ pt double cream.
1 green pepper — de-seeded and sliced

Fry the onion, mushrooms and peppers in butter gently till soft, but not coloured. Add the sultanas, brandy, cream and herbs, simmer to thicken slightly. Serve with steaks grilled to taste. This sauce can be added to fresh cooked pasta shapes and served with grilled fresh salmon or tuna.

Mulled Plums

$2^1/_2$ lbs plums (can be more if preferred)
$^1/_2$ pt red wine 2 bay leaves
$^1/_2$ tsp ground cinnamon or 1 cinnamon stick
2 cloves

1 star anais (optional)
4 cardamon pods (the seeds) or
    $^1/_4$ tsp ground cardamon
7 fl ozs honey or 7 fl ozs honey &
    water mix ($^1/_2$ & $^1/_2$)

Halve and stone plums and place a single layer in a large baking dish. Put all the remaining ingredients into a saucepan and bring to the boil. Pour over the plums and tightly cover with a lid or foil. Bake for I hour in a low oven at gas mark 3. Serve with cream or crème fraiche.

Pineapple Suchard

1 x 15 gms tinned pineapple pieces
2 ozs (63 gms) butter
2 ozs (63 gms) sugar

2 ozs (63 gms) plain flour
2 eggs 1 pt milk
4 ozs (125 gms) caster sugar

Drain the pineapple reserving the juice, put the pineapple in a dish approx 8" round lightly buttered. Melt butter and sugar gently in a saucepan. Mix flour to paste with pineapple juice, add the milk and whisk in the egg yolks. Add to the pan with the sugar and butter mix. Stir until thickened, and then pour over the pineapple. Bake for 5 minutes in a preheated oven at gas mark 5 (375°F, 190°C). Whisk egg whites till firm, and then fold in the caster sugar. Spread on to the cooked pineapple mixture. Bake for 30 minutes in preheated oven at gas mark 1 (200°F, 100°C) until light golden brown. Serve hot or cold.

Hob-Knob Lemon Slice

8 ozs Hob-Nobs — crushed
3 ozs butter — melted
$^1/_2$ pt double cream

1 can condensed milk
Juice and rind of 4 lemons

8-inch loose-base tin. Mix crushed biscuits with melted butter, press into base of tin. Whisk cream, condensed milk, juice and rind of lemon till thick, pour onto biscuit base. Chill for 2-3 hours. Serve with fresh strawberries.

Fruit Tart

Pastry: 6 ozs plain flour
4 ozs melted butter

$1^1/_2$ ozs icing sugar
1 tbls cold water

Filling: 1 carton of fresh custard
Choose any fruit in season
to decorate

1 tub of mascarpone cheese

Melt butter in a bowl and stir in flour, sugar and water to make soft dough. Press the dough into an 8-inch flan tin, prick the base and cook for 20 minutes at gas mark 5 (190°C). Remove base when crisp and golden and leave to cool. In a clean bowl add mascraphone cheese and custard, whip together until smooth and spoon into the flan base. Decorate with fruit in season and enjoy.

Caramelised Orange Trifle with Madeira

Serves 4-6.

4 trifle sponges
2-3 level tbls Seville orange marmalade
$^1/_2$ pt/275 mls freshly squeezed orange juice
2 medium bananas
1 x 298 gms tin mandarin oranges in light syrup — drained

1 x 135 gms pack orange flavoured jelly
broken into cubes
3 fl ozs/75 mls Madeira or sherry —
preferably dry
$1^1/_2$ tbls Vahiné Caramel Nature sauce

Topping: 1 x 250 gms tub Mascarpone, at room temperature
2 ozs/50 gms almonds, skin on, lightly toasted
under the grill and roughly chopped

1 vanilla pod 400 gms fresh ready-made
custard

You will need a 3 pt (1.75 litre) glass bowl. First of all, split the sponges in half lengthways, spread each half with marmalade, then reform them into sandwiches. Spread the top of each sandwich with marmalade then cut each one across into three, then arrange the pieces in the base of the glass bowl. Now make a few stabs in the sponges with a skewer and carefully pour the Madeira over all of them, distributing it as evenly as you can, then drizzle the caramel sauce over that. Leave to one side for the sponges to soak it all up. Place the cubes of jelly in a measuring jug, add 5 fl ozs (150 mls) of boiling water and stir until they have dissolved. Then top up with the orange juice to make 1 pt (570 mls) of liquid and give a good stir. Next, arrange the drained orange segments in among the sponge cakes in the trifle bowl, tipping it from side to side to make sure that all the Madeira has soaked in. Now slice the bananas thinly and scatter these into the bowl as well. Pour the jelly mixture over the fruit and, once the jelly has cooled, cover the dish with cling film and transfer it to the fringe for 3–4 hours or until the jelly has set.

Meanwhile, put the mascarpone in a mixing bowl. Then split the vanilla pod lengthways and, using the end of a tea spoon, scoop out the seeds into the bowl. Beat the mascarpone to soften it and the add the custard and whisk them together. Now cover this with cling film and also chill in the fridge. Once the jelly has set, top the trifle with the mascarpone custard mixture, cover and return to the fridge until required. Serve chilled, with the nuts scattered all over.

Boston Cheesecake

Base: 8 ozs digestive biscuits — crushed   3 ozs butter — melted 1 oz sugar

Topping: 2 ozs butter   2 ozs caster sugar
         8 ozs cream cheese   1 tsp vanilla essence
         $1/2$ pt double cream   1 x 10 ozs can crushed pineapple — drained

8-inch loose bottom flan tin. Mix crushed biscuits and sugar with butter and press into flan tin. Cream butter, sugar, cream cheese and essence together until smooth, spread over biscuit base. Whip cream and fold in pineapple. Spread over cheese mixture. Chill for a few hours before serving.

Frozen Chocolate Rum and Raisin Cake

Base: 3 ozs margarine   8 ozs plain chocolate digestive biscuits — crushed

Filling: 2 ozs raisins   4 tbls dark rum or brandy
         2 ozs caster sugar   6 ozs plain chocolate
         3 egg yolks $1/2$ pt double cream
         5 tbls water

Melt butter and add the crushed biscuits. Line the base of a 9-inch spring-form tin with the mixture. Soak the raisins in the rum or brandy. Add 5 tbls of water to the sugar and boil rapidly for 4 minutes. Whisk egg

40

Custard Cream Biscuits and Ginger Biscuits
(see p.64)

yolks and pour over the cooled syrup, whisking all the time. Add rum drained from the raisins. Melt the chocolate and add to the mixture, then cool. Add whipped cream and raisins. Pour into the tin. Freeze. Allow about 2 hours out of the freezer before eating. Serve with single cream or ice cream.

Raspberry Gateau

2 packets trifle sponges	4 ozs caster sugar
4 ozs unsalted butter	4 ozs ground almonds
Almond essence	Sherry or Cointreau
2 tins raspberries	2-3 tbls double cream

For decoration: Whipped double cream   Frozen or fresh raspberries
Grated chocolate.

Line a 2 lbs loaf tin with greaseproof paper. Split the trifle sponges and line base and sides of tin. Sprinkle with sherry or Cointreau. Beat together the butter and sugar until fluffy. Work in the almonds and almond essence. Add sufficient cream to make a creamy mixture. Add a layer of the creamed mixture to the tin, then a layer of raspberries and a layer of sponge. Sprinkle with liqueur. Repeat layers, finishing with sponge. Freeze in tin.

Thaw out, turn out on to plate, cover with whipped cream and decorate with raspberries and chocolate.

Lemon Cotswold Cheesecake

Base: 6 ozs butter   12 ozs digestive biscuits

Filling: 1 lemon jelly   6 fl ozs water
8 ozs caster sugar   7 fl ozs double cream
2 lemons   6 ozs cream cheese

Dissolve the jelly in water and add zest of lemons and lemon juice. Mix cream cheese and sugar, beat in the jelly and lemon mixture. Whisk cream and fold into the mixture. Melt butter and add crumbled biscuits and press into a loose bottomed tin (11-inch diameter). Pour mixture onto base and chill in fridge.

JW's Christmas Pudding

8 ozs shredded suet	4 ozs cherries (quartered)
1 tsp mixed spice	2 ozs ground almonds
$1/4$ tsp nutmeg	2 ozs mixed peel — finely chopped
$1/4$ tsp ground cinnamon	Grated rind of 1 orange
Grated rind of 1 lemon	4 ozs self-raising flour

1 apple — peeled, cored & grated
1 carrot (grated)
4 standard eggs
5 fl ozs barley wine
5 fl ozs stout
4 tbls rum

1 lb muscavado sugar
5 ozs white breadcrumbs
8 ozs sultanas
8 ozs raisins
1¼ lbs currants

Put suet, spices, flour, breadcrumbs and sugar in a bowl, mixing in each ingredient thoroughly before adding the next. Gradually mix in all the fruit, ground almonds, cherries and peel. Mix well. In a separate bowl beat up the eggs, mix in the stout, rum, barley wine, grated apple and carrot. Mix thoroughly. Pour over all the dry ingredients and stir until well mixed. The mixture should fall from the spoon when sharply tapped against the side of the bowl. If required, use a little more stout to get the 'dropping consistency'. When thoroughly mixed, cover with cling film and a cloth and leave overnight.

Next day grease the pudding basins (either 2 x 2 pt basins or 4 x 1 pt basins) well with butter and fill to the top. Cover each pudding with a double thickness of buttered greaseproof paper. Make a pleat in the paper to allow the pudding to rise. Tie securely with string and steam for 8 hours (keep an eye on the water to make sure it does not boil dry). When cooked allow to cool, remove paper and replace with fresh greaseproof paper, cover with cling film and then foil. Store in a cool dry place. When ready to use, re-cover with a double thickness of buttered greaseproof paper and steam for a further 2 hours.

Bishop's Cake

8 ozs sugar
8 ozs butter
8 ozs self-raising flour
3 eggs
4 ozs candied peel

4 ozs cherries
2 ozs nuts (I use pecan)
2 ozs angelica (when I have been unable to buy angelica
    I have used green and yellow cherries instead)
2 ozs ground almonds

Beat together the butter and sugar. When creamed, gradually add beaten eggs and flour alternately. Stir in all the other ingredients. Put the mixture into two lined 2 lbs loaf tins and bake in the centre of the oven 170°C for one hour or until firm to touch. Can be sliced with butter or eaten without.

Humming Bird Cake

9 ozs self-raising flour
½ tsp salt
2 medium eggs — beaten
2 small ripe bananas — mashed

10 ozs unrefined light muscavado sugar
¼ tsp mixed spice or cinnamon
8 fl ozs oil (corn or sunflower)
1 tsp vanilla essence or 2-3 drops of vanilla extract

6 ozs tin of crushed pineapple
with juice

Topping: 3¹/2 ozs butter   1 tsp vanilla essence or 2-3 drops of vanilla extract
6 ozs cream cheese — full fat   11 ozs unrefined golden icing sugar — sieved

Mix the dry ingredients together. Add the oil, vanilla, pineapple, banana and eggs. Carry on mixing to a batter. Pour into a greased and lined round cake tin (2 x 8-inches) and bake for 30–35 minutes at gas mark 4 (180°C). Cream the butter and cream cheese together with the vanilla. Add the icing sugar and spread on each layer. Decorate with flowers (optional).

Apple Cake

8 ozs self-raising flour   4 ozs granulated sugar
4 ozs butter   2 eggs
3 or 4 Bramley apples   A little milk

Put flour, sugar and chopped butter into a bowl. Slice in the apples, stir in beaten eggs and enough milk to make a stiff batter. Place mixture in a 7-inch square tin and cook for approximately 45 minutes at 180°C. Serve warm with Devonshire clotted cream (naturally), if not available, serve with double cream. Also delicious with custard. If there are any leftovers, the cake can be enjoyed cold.

   Tip: The butter sometimes has a tendency to spill over so it is recommended that you place the cake tin on a baking tray.

Boiling Water Tea Bread

2 ozs margarine   4 ozs light brown sugar
8 ozs self raising flour   1 tsp mixed spice
1 tsp bicarbonate of soda   ¹/2 lb mixed fruit — any combination
1 egg

Mix all the ingredients together, add 1 cup (7 fluid ozs) of boiling water and mix well. Pour into tin (1 x 2 lbs loaf tin — lined and greased). Cook for 1-1¹/2 hours at gas mark 5 (375°F/180°C).

Healthy Bran Cake

1 mug of All Bran   1 mug of sultanas
1 mug of skimmed milk   ¹/2 mug of demerara sugar
1 mug of self-raising flour

Boiling Water Tea Bread
(see p.43)

Mix All Bran, sultanas, sugar and milk together and leave to absorb for 1 hour. Mix in the flour, put in a lined loaf tin and bake for 50 minutes at gas mark 4 (350°F/180°C).

American Candied Fruit Cake

1 cup plain flour — sifted
1/4 tsp salt
1 cup glace cherries
2 eggs — beaten
4 cups pecan halves

1 tsp baking powder — sifted
1 1/4 cups pineapple (ready to eat packet)
1 3/4 cups dates — chopped
1/2 cup caster sugar
Brandy to soak cake after cooking

Add flour, baking powder and salt to pineapple, cherries and dates, toss to coat fruit with flour. Add eggs, sugar then nuts, mix well and pour into prepared tin (14 x 4 1/2 inch or 2 x 2 lbs loaf tins — greased and lined). Bake 1 1/2 hours at gas mark 2 (275°F/130°C). Cool, then turn out. Wrap in foil to keep, feed it with brandy to enrich the flavour.
   Make the cake at the beginning of November to eat at Christmas.

Scottish Oatcakes

8 ozs oatmeal (medium or pinhead)
1 tsp salt
2 rounded tsp sugar
100 mls water

4 ozs plain flour
1 rounded tsp baking powder
2 1/2 ozs butter

Rub together well the butter and all dry ingredients until like breadcrumbs. Mix in the water, roll out and cut. Bake in a hot oven 170–180°C for 15–20mins. Then eat and enjoy!

Peach Liqueur

500 gms peaches
2 pieces of mace

300 gms granulated sugar
750 mls brandy

Halve, stone and slice the peaches, crack the stones and remove the kernel. Arrange the peaches and sugar, in layers in a glass jar, add mace and brandy. Shake every day for 3 weeks. Strain through a cheesecloth, bottle, seal and lable. Leave for 1 month before drinking. Very good if added to a sauce for pork.
   This recipe can also be made using apricots.

Blackberry Liqueur

500 gms blackberries

750 mls dry white wine

500 gms sugar

750 mls gin

Put sugar and white wine in a saucepan, heat until the sugar is melted. Add blackberries and boil. Add the gin when cooling. Cool, pour into jar, shake every day for 30 days. Strain through a cheesecloth, bottle and label. Leave 1 week before using.

This recipe can also be made using redcurrants or blackcurrants.

Elderflower Cordial

$1^{1}/2$ lbs granulated sugar

$1^{3}/4$ pt boiling water

25 gms citric acid

Mix the above together. Add 15–20 clean flower heads and 2 sliced lemons. Leave for 48 hours, stirring occasionally. Strain through cheesecloth, bottle and label. Use after 1 week.

Piccalilli

2 medium cauliflowers

1 lb onion

12 ozs demerara sugar

$1/2$ oz turmeric

2 pt white pickling vinegar

3 cucumbers

2 lbs pickling onions

1 oz dry mustard

6 tbls plain flour (level)

3 tbls salt

Break the cauliflower into small sprigs. Peel and dice the cucumbers. Peel and chop the onions. Peel the pickling onions. Mixed the vegetables in a large bowl. Sprinkle with 3 level tablespoons of salt. Cover with a plate. Leave overnight.

Next day, drain vegetables thoroughly.

Sauce: Put demerara sugar, mustard, turmeric and flour into a large bowl. Blend them into a paste with some of the white pickling vinegar. Put the rest of the white pickling vinegar into a saucepan and bring slowly to the boil. Strain the boiling white pickling vinegar onto the blended ingredients, stirring all the time. Put the mustard sauce into a large pan and bring slowly to the boil. Add the drained vegetables to the mustard sauce. Bring the piccalilli to the boil and simmer for 25 mins. Fill heated jars and cover with polythene.

Old Dover House Chutney

$1^{1}/_{2}$ lbs plums (preferably Victoria)
8 ozs green/red tomatoes
8 ozs onions
4 ozs preserved ginger or 2 tsp
    of ground ginger
$1^{1}/_{2}$ tbls cooking salt

$1^{1}/_{2}$ lbs cooking apples (weighed after peeling)
1 lb stoned raisins
$1^{1}/_{2}$ lbs demerera sugar
$^{1}/_{4}$ oz garlic
$^{1}/_{4}$ oz whole chillies
1 pt malt vinegar

Wash the plums, cut in half. Chop the tomatoes roughly and place both in pan. Pass the onions, apples, raisins and ginger through a course mincer or chop, add with garlic, vinegar, salt and sugar to the pan. Tie the chillies in gauze and suspend from handle into pan. Cook slowly for 1–$1^{1}/_{2}$ hours until most of liquid has evaporated. Stir occasionally. Allow to cool. Jar and label. Keep one month before using.

Cheese Bombe and Scottish Oatcakes
(see pp.67 & 45)

Celebrities

Mushroom Soup

2 ozs butter	12 ozs mushrooms
2 ozs flour	¹/4 pt of milk

Melt butter in a saucepan, blend in flour and cook over a low heat for 2-3 minutes, stirring constantly. Gradually add the milk into the mixture which will thicken at first. Keep beating until smooth and then add the sliced mushrooms. Leave to cook until you can smell the mushroom flavour. Use enough milk to thin soup to your taste and season as required. Liquidise until smooth. Pour through a sieve into a serving bowl. Garnish with fried mushrooms.

Prawn Hot-pot Soup

8 ozs peeled prawns	2 dried red chillies
4 ozs any white fish	4 tsp fennel seeds
2 ozs fish stock	1 chopped onion

Peel the prawns and the onion. Put the shells and the onion into a saucepan and cover with boiling water. Leave to simmer for 15 minutes. Crush the dried red chillies and fennel seeds in a pestle and mortar. Add to the stock and cook for a further 10 minutes, then strain.

Add the prawns and white fish to the stock and reheat for a minute, without boiling. Sprinkle fresh coriander over and serve immediately.

Broccoli and Leek Soup

2 ozs butter	3 leeks
1 chopped onion	1¹/2 pts chicken stock
12 ozs broccoli	

Melt butter in a pan, add the chopped onion. Meanwhile roughly chop up the broccoli stalk and white part of the leek. Add to the saucepan and leave to sweat for 4-5 minutes. Add the chicken stock and cook through for a further 10 minutes or until the vegetables are soft.

Chop the florets and the clean green leaves of the leeks. Add to the boiling stock and cook for another 10-20 minutes. Put in the liquidiser — strain through sieve to serve. Garnish with a sprinkling of fried ham.

Chicken Consommé with Tarragon and Quails Eggs
Serves 6.

3 pts good chicken stock
8 ozs mixed vegetables
8 ozs onion (one whole onion)
3 quails eggs per person

1 chicken carcass or the equivalent in bones
Fresh tarragon
4 egg whites

Place the stock in a thick bottomed pan and whisk in the egg whites. Add the mixed vegetables (diced) to the stock, the fresh tarragon and the chicken carcass or chicken bones. Wash the onion and trim the root, leaving the skin on, cut in half and burn, cut side down, on the hot plate, add to the stock (the burnt onion will add a warm amber colour to the soup). Place on the hot plate and bring slowly to the boil, stirring occasionally. When boiling, stir once more then allow to simmer very gently for one hour. Strain through a muslin cloth. De-grease if necessary and correct seasoning. Poach the quails eggs for 3 minutes.

To serve place 3 quails eggs (previously warmed in a small amount of consommé) into individual tureens and pour over the chicken consommé. Garnish with a very thin slice of lemon and one or two leaves of tarragon.

Broad Bean and Thyme Risotto
Serves 4.

350 gms young broad beans shelled (1 kg in their pods)
285 gms risotto rice (arborio or carnaroli for example)
1 ltr light vegetable stock
85 gms unsalted butter

1 small onion peeled and chopped
150 mls white wine
6 sprigs of thyme
60 gms freshly grated Parmesan

Thyme Cream:

3 heaped dessertspoons crème fraiche

2 heaped tsps chopped thyme

Bring a large pan of water to the boil and cook the beans (allow about 6 minutes for fresh ones). Cool under running water, skin and reserve them. Heat the stock up to simmering point on the stove, and keep it on a low heat while cooking the risotto. Heat 50grams. of the butter in a heavy-bottomed pan and sweat the onion over a low heat until translucent and soft; it must not colour. Add the rice and cook for 1 to 2 minutes. Pour in the wine and continue to cook until the liquid has been absorbed. Add the thyme sprigs and start to pour in ladles of simmering stock — at no stage should the rice be flooded. It will take 25minutes to cook. Stir in the parmesan and the remaining butter. Remove the thyme sprigs and add the beans to heat through. Adjust seasoning and serve with a spoonful of thyme cream in the centre.

Bacon Pancakes

3 ozs plain flour
1/2 pt of milk
2 eggs
Salt and black pepper

1 1/2 teaspoons mixed herbs
1/2 lb streaky bacon
1 oz dripping

Sift flour into a bowl and stir in half the milk. Add the eggs and remaining milk and whisk until the batter is smooth and light. Season with salt and ground black pepper and mix in the herbs. Remove the rind and cut the bacon rashers in half inch wide strips. Fry in fat over medium heat for 3–4 minutes. Measure two tablespoons of the fat into a heated fireproof dish, add drained bacon and pour over the pancake batter. Bake in the centre of a pre-heated oven at gas mark 4 (180°C/350°F) for 30 minutes or until set. Serve with grilled tomatoes.

Champ

This is a delicious Irish speciality which is simple and quick to cook. It should be served with plenty of melted butter drizzling down — but the health conscious can reduce this. Serves 4.

900 gms/2 lbs floury potatoes
Spring onions
25 gms/1 oz butter

4 tbls milk
Salt and freshly ground black pepper
Knobs of butter to serve

In separate pans, boil the potatoes and onions in lightly salted boiling water until tender (the onions will cook for a much shorter time than the potatoes). Drain both and mash the potatoes in a bowl with the butter and the milk. Add the onions to the potatoes and mix in with some seasoning. Heap into a bowl and make a hollow in the centre of the mash. Add extra knobs of butter and serve immediately.

Thai Pasta and Seafood Salad

$^{1}/_{4}$ cup peanut butter

$^{1}/_{3}$ cup cider vinegar
2 tbls sugar
1 tsp minced garlic
2 $^{1}/_{4}$ cup chilled cooked shrimp and scallops
1 cup cilantro leaves, chopped
7 cup chilled cooked pasta

3 med pickling cucumbers halved lengthwise, seeded and thinly sliced crosswise
2 medium red bell peppers, cored and sliced thin
$^{1}/_{2}$ cup sliced scallions
$^{1}/_{4}$ cup hot water
2 tbls soy sauce
1 tbls ground fresh ginger

Whisk peanut butter and hot water in large bowl until smooth. Whisk in vinegar, soy sauce, sugar, ginger root and garlic. Add remaining ingredients; toss to mix. Makes 12 cups, 6 servings.

Roast Duckling

You need a half duckling per person. For two people you would need a duck weighing about 4 lbs, as well as some salt and freshly ground black pepper to season. The secret is not to put any fat on the duck, just prick it all over with a skewer, going deep into the flesh, and put a rack in the roasting tin. Pre-heat the oven to

(425°F/220°C) and place the tin on a highish shelf in the oven. After 20 minutes, turn the heat down to 350°F/180°C), then all you have to do is leave it alone for two hours.

For the gravy, simmer some chicken stock with giblets from the duck for quite a while to give it a good flavour. When the duck is ready, remove all the fat except for a dessert spoon and the nice brown bits in the roasting tin. Then add one dessertspoonful of flour and cook the roux for a few minutes to brown it, add the strained stock and stir until smooth. Then add some red wine and two dessertspoons of redcurrant jelly, which I feel gives it a nice flavour. The result is a lovely, aromatic dish. Enjoy!

Turkey Meatballs

225 gms (8 ozs) minced turkey
55 gms (2 ozs) fresh breadcrumbs
1 onion — finely chopped
1 egg white

$1/2$ tablespoon olive oil
Salt and freshly ground black pepper
1 heaped teaspoon paprika

Preheat the oven to gas mark 6 (200°C/400°F). Heat the oil in a pan and then add the onion. Cook gently for 10 minutes and add the paprika once the onions are softened. Fry for 30 seconds. Transfer to a food processor and blend with the turkey, breadcrumbs and egg white and season well. Form the mixture into 8 meatballs. Place the meatballs on a non-stick baking sheet and bake in the oven for 20 minutes. Then remove from the oven and transfer the meatballs into any sauce for the last 15 minutes' cooking time.

St David's Chicken

4 boneless chicken breasts — approx 100 gms/4 ozs each
100 gms/4 ozs smoked back bacon — rinded
1 large leek — trimmed
50 gms/2 ozs butter

1 tbls chopped fresh parsley
2 tbls clear honey
150 mls ($1/4$ pt) chicken stock
Salt and pepper

Wash chicken and pat dry. Dice bacon and slice leek. Melt butter in a large frying pan or wok. Add chicken and bacon and fry for 10 minutes, turning frequently. Add leeks. Stir in honey and stock and season to taste. Reduce heat and simmer for 20 minutes, or until the chicken is cooked. Adjust seasoning and stir in the parsley. Remove chicken from pan with a slotted spoon. Cut each piece diagonally into four and fan out on a serving plate. Spoon over sauce and serve.

Roast Beef & Yorkshire Pudding
Serves 8–10.

1 x 3-rib-bone forerib of beef, oven ready,
approximate weight 3 kgs

1 lb shallots — peeled
Cooking oil

St David's Chicken
(See p.52)

(8 lbs) or a boned and rolled rib from
the same cut, approximate weight
2-25 kgs (4¹/2 –5¹/2 lbs)

Salt and pepper

Pre-heat the oven to gas mark 5 (190°C/375°F). Heat a roasting pan with 2–3 tablespoons of cooking oil. Season the beef rib generously with salt and pepper. Place in the hot pan and colour and seal on all sides. Roast in the preheated oven, allowing 25 minutes per 450 gms (1 lb), whether it is on or off the bone, for a medium finish. It is important to baste the beef every 15 minutes to ensure all round flavour and seasoning. Halfway through the cooking time, turn the joint over, sprinkling the shallots around the pan. Once the cooking time is complete, remove the beef from the oven and roasting tray. Cover with foil and leave to rest for 10 minutes before carving.

Yorkshire Pudding — (makes up to 24 puddings)

225 gms (8 ozs) plain flour
Pinch of salt
3 eggs

300–450 mls milk
Oil
Lard or dripping for cooking

Pre-heat the oven to gas mark 7 (220°C/425°F). The quantity will fill 10–12 10 cm (4-inch) individual tins, approximately two 12-pudding-mould trays or 1 medium roasting tin, approximately 20 x 25 cm (8" x 10"). The batter can be made and used immediately, but better given ¹/2–1 hour resting time. Sift the flour with the salt. Add the eggs. Whisk in 300mls (¹/2 pt) of the milk. This will give you a thick batter that works very well. To check for the perfect consistency, simply lift a spoon in and out. The batter should hold and coat the back of a spoon. If it seems to have congealed after resting simply add more of the remaining milk until that consistency is found. The batter is now ready to cook. Oil or grease your chosen tin(s) fairly generously. These can then be heated in the oven until almost smoking. For individual tins or mould trays, fill each to almost full. For the medium roasting tray, just add all the batter. Bake in the pre-heated oven for 25–30 minutes for individual/mould trays). An extra 5–10 minutes may still be needed for a crispy finish. A roasting tray will take 45 minutes to 1 hour.

Meatball & Tomato Sauce

500 gms minced beef
3 cloves garlic, chopped
2 tbls chopped fresh mint & parsley
Tomato Sauce: *400 gms can of chopped tomatoes*
1 fresh red or green chilli, deseeded
and chopped*
1 tbls fresh parsley, basil or coriander,
chopped
1 large onion, very finely chopped

Salt and black pepper
1 egg
2 tbls olive oil
2 tbls olive oil
1 chicken or vegetable stock cube

2 tbls white wine

Salt & freshly ground black pepper

* omit the chilli from tomato sauce if you do not like your food too hot.

Put the tomatoes and their juice in a wok with the crumbled stock cube, wine, onion, olive oil and chilli. Add the herbs, a little salt & pepper, bring to simmering point, cover and let it bubble away for 5–10 minutes. Mix together the mincemeat, garlic, fresh herbs and salt & pepper. Break the egg into it and mix it up with your hands. Form the mixture into meatballs the size of table-tennis balls. Heat the oil in a frying pan and fry the meatballs gently for 7–10 minutes. When they are cooked through, add them to the tomato sauce and serve with spaghetti, cooked *al dente*.

Spaghetti Bolognese

To serve 4.

1^1/2 lbs/675 gms extra lean minced beef	^{1}/2 pt/300 mls beef stock
8 ozs/225 gms chicken livers	1 glass red wine
2 large onions, chopped	Large pinch mixed herbs
2 cloves garlic, chopped	Salt and freshly ground black pepper
Oil — for frying	Splash of dry sherry
2 tbls /30 mls tomato purée	Fresh parmesan cheese, to serve
425 gms can chopped tomatoes	

Heat the oil in a large pan, add the onion and garlic. Fry over a low heat until softened. Add the minced beef and chicken livers, increase the heat and cook until brown. Stir in the tomato purée, canned tomatoes and herbs. Add the beef stock and wine gradually. Season and bring to the boil. Decrease the heat and simmer for about 1 hour until rich brown in colour. Stirring and adding more stock or wine if necessary. Just before serving add a splash of sherry. Serve with spaghetti and a sprinkling of freshly grated parmesan cheese.

Lamb Hotpot

8 chump chops	2 large carrots
3 large potatoes	1 medium onion
2 large leeks	^{1}/2 pt of lamb stock seasoning

Peel and slice one potato thinly and cover the bottom of a large casserole dish with it. Roughly chop the onion, cut leeks into one inch pieces, cut carrots into thin slices, and place these on top of the sliced potato in the dish. Season well. Cut as much fat off the chops as you can and put the chops on top of the vegetables in the dish. Season again. Pour stock in. Cut the remaining 2 potatoes into large chunks and place on top of the chops & season. Cover with greaseproof paper and a tight fitting lid. Cook in the oven at 200°C or gas mark 5 for 2^1/2 hours. Serve with freshly chopped parsley sprinkled on top.

Thai Green Curry Paste

The green of this curry paste comes from the fresh coriander leaves. Like all plant materials, the natural chlorophyl (green colour) oxidises in air, fading rapidly on picking and cooking. Although this paste will last for up to a week in the refrigerator, it should be used within 2 days for maximum impact, colour and flavour. It is best for the clear, hot, sour/sweet curries much beloved of the Thais.

15 green chillies, chopped
3 cloves garlic, peeled and roughly chopped
1 tbls chopped galangal or ginger
1 tbls sugar
2 tbls fish sauce
1 tsp ground coriander
4 tbls or 1 bunch of fresh coriander
    leaves, chopped juice and grated
    rind of 2 limes

4 spring onions or 1 large onion, peeled
    and chopped
1 tbls oil
1 tsp blachan (shrimp paste) or 2 tsp
    dried shrimps
3 stalks of lemon grass, crushed
3 fresh kaffir lime leaves (optional)

Combine all the ingredients and liquidise or process to a smooth paste in a food processor. This can be added to any ingredients you like, for example lightly fried strips of breast of chicken, or strips of beef, green and red peppers and onions, baby sweet corn or anything else that takes your fancy. Serve with Thai fragrant rice.

Potato Cakes

Mash as much potato as you like with salt, pepper, a little milk and butter — the final consistency should be a little softer than normal mash, but not over-soft. Wait until it is quite cool, then add a cup of self raising flour, if you only have plain, that'll do! It will still be quite a bit doughy and sticky, that's fine, but you will need a fair bit of flour on your hands to shape the mixture into balls, put them on a baking tray and flatten down into circles about 1cm thick and 8cm round. Put the baking tray at the top of a fairly hot oven (200°C) and bake for 10–15 mins, or until golden brown. Serve them either hot or cold, spread with butter.

Marmalade Ice Cream

3 large eggs
$^3/_4$ pt double cream
75 gms sugar
1 tbls Cointreau

2 tbls orange juice
3 tbls dark marmalade
1tbls brandy

Take three mixing bowls, put the egg yolks in one, the egg whites in another and the cream in the third. Put 50 gms sugar in with the egg yolks and beat till thick and light. Heat the marmalade with the brandy, cool slightly and mix with the yolks. Add the orange juice and beat again. Beat the cream with the sugar until stiff.

Fruit Scones
(see p.58)

Combine the yolk mixture, adding Cointreau. Whip the whites until they form peaks, fold lightly into the mixture and freeze. Serve with a bowl of strawberries and sliced oranges.

Bara Brith (Welsh cake-bread)

1 pkt of dried mixed fruit
4 ozs demerara sugar
1 cup warm strong tea
$^{1}/_{4}$ tsp mixed spice

1 egg, and if necessary a little milk
1 tbls marmalade
8 ozs self-raising flour

Pour the warm tea over the dried fruit and sugar and allow to stand for a few hours, or overnight, to swell the fruit. Add the beaten egg and other ingredients to the flour and mix well together to a dropping consistency and put to bake in a loaf tin on gas mark 3 for about $1^{1}/_{4}$ hours. delicious with home-made jam for tea.

Fruit Scones

$^{1}/_{2}$ lb plain flour
1 level tsp bicarbonate of soda
2 level tsp cream of tartar
$^{1}/_{2}$ tsp salt

2 ozs butter
1 oz caster sugar
2 ozs sultanas or raisins
$^{1}/_{4}$ pt milk approx

Sift flour, raising agent, soda, salt and sugar into bowl. Rub in butter until very fine, then add the sultanas or raisons. Pour in liquid, knead lightly. Roll out and cut into rounds with 2-inch cutter. Bake near the top in oven 230°F. (450°C) for 10-15mins. Serve at once with jam and cream— delicious!

Fresh Cream Truffles (with or without booze or ginger)

These last at least 2 weeks in the fridge. Makes approximately 25.

200 mls/7 fl ozs double cream
200 gms/7 ozs good quality plain chocolate
15-30 mls /1-2 tbls spirits/liqueur and
   finely chopped stem ginger (both optional)

15 mls (1 tbls) sifted cocoa powder
1 Cadbury's Flake

Place the cream in a saucepan and heat until boiling. Break chocolate into pieces and pour on hot cream, add the alcohol and/or ginger if required. Stir until chocolate has melted then beat with an electric whisk until the mixture is cold and stiff (approx. 8-10 minutes). Chill mixture for an hour or until firm enough to shape. Use a melon baler or teaspoon to shape approx 25 truffles. Roll half in the cocoa and half in crumbled Flake.

Menu Suggestion 1

STARTER: Melon and Avocado Salad with Mint Dressing

Salad: Cut 1 melon, remove seeds. Remove the flesh with a melon baller. Remove stones from 3 avocados and remove the flesh with a melon baller. Peel and dice $1/2$ cucumber, mix melon, avocado and cucumber.

Mint dressing:
2 tbls caster sugar	2 tbls wine vinegar
6 tbls olive oil	1 tsp made mustard
2 tsp melted mint jelly	

Mix the dressing ingredients together in a jar and shake well. Combine salad and dressing and serve in individual glasses. Garnish with fresh mint leaves.

MAIN COURSE: Duck with Cranberry and Port

6 duck breasts	$1/2$ pt port
3 red onions — peeled and quartered	Pinch of ground cloves and cinnamon
2 tbls oil	

Sauce:
1 x 5 ozs jar cranberry sauce	1 pt cranberry juice
$1/2$ pt cheap port (ruby wine)	1 tbls cornflour

Pat duck skin dry. Fry red onion and put into casserole dish. Dust duck well with seasoned flour and fry till golden, add to casserole, add cloves and $1/2$ pt of port. Cook in oven gas mark 6 (400°F/200°C) for 45 minutes. Mix cranberry juice, cheap port and cranberry sauce and heat, thicken with cornflour mixed with a little cranberry juice. Serve duck with red onions on a bed of creamed potatoes with spring onions, and then surround with the sauce.

DESSERT: Cheshire Cheescake

BASE:
8 ozs crushed digestive biscuits	1 tbls caster sugar
4 ozs melted butter	

Mix together and press into buttered 8-inch loose based flan tin. Bake for 5 minutes at gas mark 4 350°F/180°C. Allow to cool.

CHEESECAKE:
6 ozs caster sugar	2 dsp custard powder
8 ozs grated Cheshire cheese (finely in processor)	
Rind of 1 lemon	1 tbls lemon juice
2 eggs — beaten	5 ozs double cream

Mix all ingredients together and pour onto base, cook for 30–40 minutes at gas mark 4 (350°F/180°C). Allow to cool for 15 minutes.

TOPPING:	10 ozs soured cream	1 tsp vanilla essence
	1 tbls caster sugar	

Mix together and pour over cheesecake. Bake for 15 minutes at gas mark 7 (425°F/220°C). Serve slightly warm.

Other cheeses can be used — cranberry and wenslydale or lemon and stilton for example.

Menu Suggestion 2

STARTER: Three Fish Paté

Line 6 ramekins or a 1 lb loaf tin with cling film. Lay slices of smoked salmon (approx. 4ozs) to line the ramekins or tin.

Filling 1: 4 ozs smoked trout — skinned and boned 	*2 ozs softened butter*
2 ozs soft cream cheese 	*Juice of ½ lemon, seasoning*

Blend in food processor till smooth. Divide between ramekins or tin for first layer.

Filling 2: 4 ozs smoked mackerel 	*2 ozs softened butter*
2 ozs soft cream cheese 	*2½ fluid ozs sweet cider reduced by*
Seasoning 	*boiling to 1½ fl ozs*

Blend in food processor till smooth and spread over smoked trout in containers.

Filling 3. 4 ozs smoked salmon (trimming will be OK) 	*2 ozs softened butter*
2 ozs cream cheese 	*½ tsp tomato purée*
Juice of ½ lemon

Blend in food processor till smooth and spread over smoked mackerel. Cover with cling film and chill over night. Turn out to serve or slice if made in loaf tin. Serve on a bed of mixed leaves with French dressing and lemon slices.

MAIN COURSE: Nerja Chicken

6 chicken fillets 	*2 tbls white wine*
Rind of 2 lemons — removed with potato peeler and finely shredded.

SAUCE: ½ pt white wine 	*Juice of 2 lemons*
1 tbls honey 	*1 tbls cornflour*
½ lb white seedless grapes — peeled

Bake fillets sprinkled with white wine and lemon rind, covered in foil in a buttered dish for 25 minutes at gas

Three Fish Paté
(see p.60)

mark 4 (350°F/180°C).

SAUCE: Heat wine, honey and lemon juice. Mix cornflour with a little cold water and add to wine etc. to thicken. Add grapes just before serving.

Serve chicken with lemon rind topping surrounded by sauce.

DESSERT: Caribbean Chocolate Pots

3 ozs raisins — soaked in 3 tablespoons dark rum	$^3/_4$ pt single cream
6 ozs dark chocolate broken into pieces	3 egg yolks
2 tbls brandy	

Spoon the raisins into 6 ramekins or glasses. Heat single cream till simmering, remove from heat and add chocolate, stir until melted. Add egg yolks and beat gently. Add brandy. Pour over the raisins. Chill overnight. Sprinkle with icing sugar before serving.

Menu Suggestion 3
STARTER: Peach & Cheese Salad

Mixed leaves and French dressing	2 ozs very strong cheddar cheese — grated
2 ozs softened butter	6 tinned peach halves
4 ozs cream cheese	2 tbls caster sugar
4 tbls lemon juice	Paprika

Mix grated cheddar and butter in food processor until smooth, fill peaches with cheese mixture and set on a bed of mixed leaves lightly dressed with french dressing. Top with mixture of cream cheese, sugar and lemon juice, mixed until smooth. Sprinkle with paprika before serving.

MAIN COURSE: Bray Salmon

6 salmon fillets	2 tbls lemon juice
$^1/_2$ cucumber — peel, de-seed and dice	3 ozs butter
Juice of 2 lemons	1 tbls chopped fresh parsley

Bake salmon in buttered dish covered with lemon juice, covered with lid or foil for 20 minutes gas mark 4 (350°F/180°C).

SAUCE: Blanch cucumber and drain well. Melt butter in pan, when bubbling add cucumber and lemon juice. When heated add parsley. Serve with salmon.

DESSERT: Coffee & Brandy Gateaux

1 box sponge cakes

3 ozs caster sugar

2 tbls coffee essence

$^1/_2$ pt double cream

3 ozs butter

2 small eggs

$^1/_4$ pt brandy with 4 tbls water mixed

Hazelnuts to decorate

Cut each sponge cake in half, use four halves to line container, which has been pre-lined with cling wrap. Drizzle sponge with $^1/_4$ of brandy and water mixture. Cream butter and sugar till very soft and light in colour, add the beaten eggs a little at a time, mixing well between each addition, then add coffee essence. Layer this mixture onto sponge $^1/_3$ at a time and repeat process, finishing with sponge soaked with brandy. Cover with cling wrap and leave overnight lightly pressed with weights. Turn out and cover with whipped double cream and decorate with hazelnuts.

Elizabethen Pork

2 lbs diced lean pork

4 ozs chopped dates

1 large onion peeled and chopped

1 x 15 ozs tin orange segments with juice

1 bouquet garni

2 tbls corn flour

4 celery sticks chopped

4 ozs grapes

1 large apple peeled, cored and chopped

1 pt red wine

2 tbls vegetable oil

Fry pork in oil to seal. Drain and put into saucepan with all the other ingredients, except cornflour, and simmer for 1 hour. Mix corn flour with a little cold water, add and stir to slightly thicken the meat etc. This can be made in advance and reheated before serving.

Wessex Beef

$1^1/_2$ lbs braising steak cut into 1-inch cubes

1 medium onion peeled and sliced

$^3/_4$ pt cooking port

8 ozs sausage meat

2 tbls chopped parsley

Salt and pepper

1 oz plain flour

4 cloves

1 pt beef stock

2 ozs fresh bread crumbs

1 tbls redcurrant jelly

Toss meat in flour and put into casserole, add onions, cloves and season. Pour over the port and stock to cover the meat. Cover and cook at gas mark 4 (180°C/350°F) for two hours until the meat is tender. Mix sausage meat, bread crumbs and parsley together with floured hands, form into 8 balls add to casserole and continue cooking for 30 minutes uncovered, add redcurrant jelly and serve.

Aunty Emma Cake

4 ozs margarine
8 ozs self raising flour — sifted
2 tsp almond essence or grated rind
    of 1 lemon or 1 orange

4 ozs caster sugar or light brown sugar
9 ozs mixed fruit — any combination
2 eggs — beaten
$^1/_4$ pt milk

Cream margarine and sugar, add flour, eggs and milk, then mixed fruit and flavouring. Put into prepared tin (8-inch cake tin — lined), smooth the top, if liked sprinkle top with flaked almonds.
    Bake for 1 hour at gas mark 3–4 (350°F/180°C).

Ginger Biscuits

12 ozs self raising flour
4 ozs demerara sugar
3 heaped tsp ginger
4 ozs butter or margarine melted

4 ozs soft light brown sugar
$^1/_2$ tsp bicarbonate of soda
1 egg — beaten
1 heaped tbls syrup — melted

Mix all ingredients together, form into balls about the size of a walnut, cook spaced out on a greased tray. The biscuits double in size, so leave plenty of room for baking. Cook for 15 minutes at gas mark 4 (350°F/180°C). Makes approx 30 biscuits. Store in freezer or in an airtight tin.

Custard Cream Biscuits

4 ozs butter or margarine
1 egg yolk
Vanilla essence

4 ozs caster sugar
4 ozs self raising flour
4 ozs custard powder

Cream margarine and sugar till light, add all other ingredients to make dough. Roll out and cut with small round cutter. Bake on greased tray for 15–20 minutes till golden. Cool then sandwich together with vanilla butter cream. Sift with icing sugar to finish. Makes approx. 16 biscuits. Store in airtight tin.

Christmas Eve Cake

1 lb mixed fruit
6 tbls sherry grated rind and juice of 2 oranges
2 ozs chopped walnuts
5 ozs soft dark brown sugar
2 tsp mixed spice
2 level tbls apricot jam

8 stoned prunes
1 oz glace cherries — quartered
6 ozs soft butter
6 ozs plain flour
4 eggs — beaten
2 level tbls black treacle

Topping:	Apricot glaze	Glacé cherries
	Walnuts	Whole almonds
	Hazelnuts	

Put fruit, prunes, sherry and orange juice in saucepan and heat, stirring for about 8–10 minutes. Cover and leave overnight.

Next day, add cherries and walnuts to fruit and stir. Cream butter and sugar. Add sieved flour, spice and egg a little at a time. Mix in jam, treacle and then add soaked fruit etc. Mix well. Turn into prepared tin (8-inch tin — lined with greaseproof paper). Gas mark 1–2 (275-290°F 140-160°C). Bake for 1½–2 hours. This cake is paler than usual Christmas cakes. Leave to cool, then turn out to cool completely. Store for 2–3 weeks, then top with melted apricot glaze and decorate with nuts and cherries.

Victorian Salad Dressing

¹/₂ oz mustard powder or dessertspoon of made
6 ozs white sugar
¹/₂ pt malt vinegar

¹/₄ oz salt
¹/₂ pt milk
2 eggs plus 2 egg yolks

Beat eggs, sugar and mustard together, add salt, then milk and lastly vinegar. Pour into thick based saucepan and heat slowly. Cook gently (do not boil) till mixture thickens. Cool, bottle and label. Keep in a cool place.

Apple Chutney (food processor method)

3 lbs apples — peeled and cored
1 lb sultanas
2 lbs demerara sugar
¹/₂ tsp ground ginger
¹/₄ tsp chilli powder

2 lbs onions — peeled and quartered
1 lb raisins
1 ozs salt
¹/₂ oz mustard seed
1¹/₄ pt malt vinegar

Mix apples, onions, sultanas and raisins in a bowl, process in batches till chopped quite finely. Into large saucepan put sugar, salt, ginger, mustard seed, chilli, vinegar, apples etc. Bring to boil then simmer gently till rich brown in colour and thick — approximately 40 minutes. Jar and label. Keep 2 months before eating.

Whisky Cream

6 fl ozs whisky
6 tsp Camp coffee

1 tin condensed milk
¹/₂ pt double cream

Mix together well, bottle and label. Use after 1 week.

Nerja Chicken and Caribbean
Chocolate Pots
(see pp.60 & 62)